W9-CJG-924

A BEACON BIOGRAPHY

DRAKE

Tamra Orr

PURPLE TOAD
PUBLISHING

P.O. Box 631
Kennett Square, Pennsylvania 19348
www.purpletoadpublishing.com

Printing   1   2   3   4   5   6   7   8   9

A Beacon Biography

Big Time Rush
Carly Rae Jepsen
Drake
Harry Styles of One Direction
Jennifer Lawrence
Kevin Durant
Robert Griffin III (RG3)

Publisher's Cataloging-in-Publication Data
Orr, Tamra
  Drake / Tamra Orr
    p. cm. — (A beacon biography)
Includes bibliographic references and index.
ISBN: 978-1-62469-022-8 (library bound)
1. Drake, 1986–. 2. Singers — Canada — Biography — Juvenile literature.   I. Title.
  ML3930.D73 2013
  782.421649092 — dc23
                                                                                        2013934692

eBook ISBN: 9781624690273

ABOUT THE AUTHOR: Tamra Orr is a full-time author living in the Pacific Northwest with her husband, children, cat, and dog. She graduated from Ball State University in Muncie, Indiana. She has written more than 300 books about many subjects, ranging from historical events and career choices to controversial issues and celebrity biographies. On those rare occasions when she is not writing books, she is reading them. Her four kids make sure she stays current on popular music, even if she doesn't want to.

Printed by Lake Book Manufacturing, Chicago, IL

CONTENTS

Drake onstage

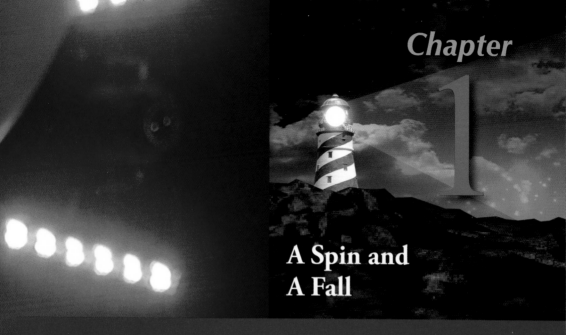

Chapter 1

A Spin and A Fall

It was a moment that Drake—and millions of his fans—will likely never forget.

As part of the America's Most Wanted tour with Lil Wayne, Drake was performing the opening lines of his number one song, "The Best I Ever Had." The Camden, New Jersey, crowd was cheering wildly as Drake combined his familiar lyrics with a quick spin. Then he crumpled to the floor.

The audience was confused. What had happened?

Drake did not get up. Four stagehands silently helped him to his feet. It was clear that he could not walk on his own. They supported him while he hobbled off the stage. Within minutes, Lil Wayne came out and took over the stage, asking the crowd to show their concern and appreciation for the injured rap artist with a round of applause.

The next night of the tour, the audience was disappointed to find that Drake would not be returning any time soon. They were shocked to find out why, however. Drake had injured a weak knee. "We had a technical difficulty yesterday," explained Lil Wayne, according to the *Examiner.* "Drake fell. . . . He's going into surgery tomorrow, so ya'll keep him in your prayers."

The audience was shocked to see Drake fall during the concert, and not get back up. He was clearly in a great deal of pain.

After years of injuring his knee while playing sports, Drake had finally pushed it too far. The spin tore his anterior cruciate ligament, or ACL. One of the major ligaments of the knee, it connects the thighbone (femur) to the lower leg bone (tibia). If it is torn, standing is almost impossible—not to mention painful. Surgery is usually the only way to repair it.

A few nights after the accident, Drake blogged about what happened to him. According to the *Examiner,* he wrote, "I am about 2 hours away from Toronto, Canada, where I will be spending the next chunk of time recovering from a surgery that I now must have. I embarked on the tour with [torn ligaments] . . . and due to the events that happened the other night, Lord only knows what other damage I have done. . . . I will forever push myself beyond the limits despite advice and recommendations given because even in this newfound success, I am still the kid who wanted this more than anything in the world."

What would the rest of the tour do without him? America's Most Wanted featured many great musical artists, but a good portion of ticketholders were huge Drake fans. Drake was determined to get back onstage, but his doctors told him no. "That's one thing I have to apologize to my fans about," he said to MTV. "It's too much of a risk [to perform], if I hit that wrong turn [during my] 30 minutes every night. If I tear my ACL again, the doctors say I might not be able to walk again. I have to be cautious." Sticking to doctors' orders, Drake sang at the closing performances of the 2009 BET Awards, but he did it sitting on stage on a stool, with a cane waiting nearby.

Slowing down in order to have surgery and recover was not easy for Drake. For years, he had been chasing a career in acting and then music. He had succeeded at both—becoming one of the first mixed-race Jewish Canadians ever to do so.

Drake's nickname, Drizzy, was spread by Lil Wayne's song "Ransom." Drake made history in 2012—he had the most #1 songs on the billboard charts in the history of rap.

Drake captivates people with his soulful voice and passionate style.

Cultural ID

It's no surprise that Drake loves music. Some might even say it's in his blood.

Aubrey Drake Graham was born on October 24, 1986, in Toronto, Ontario. His mother, Sandi, is white, Jewish, and loves music. His father, Dennis, is black. Dennis had been a drummer for the Jerry Lee Lewis band in the 1960s. Drake's uncle, Larry, played bass with the group, Sly and the Family Stone, and his other uncle, Teenie Hodges, was the lead guitarist for Al Green in the 1970s. In an interview for *Dr. Guy Presents Musiqology*, Drake added that his family has "a very deep musical background. My grandmother, who passed away in Memphis, [Tennessee,] used to babysit Louis Armstrong. [My dad] ran in that circle of great musicians, and [he] has many stories."

When Drake was only five years old, his parents divorced. He was raised by his mother in a mostly Jewish neighborhood in Toronto. His mother taught him the Jewish faith. "My mom has always made Hanukkah fun," he recalls on *Biography.com*. "When I was younger, she gave cool gifts and she'd make latkes." When

Drake was thirteen, he had a bar mitzvah, a coming-of-age ceremony for Jewish boys. It was an important life event he would later imitate in a controversial music video for one of his hit songs, "HYFR."

Because he was part white and part black, plus Canadian and Jewish, Drake straddled a number of different cultures. "At the end of the day, I consider myself a black man because I'm more immersed in black

Drake at his bar mitzvah

culture than any other," he stated to *Biography.com*. "Being Jewish is kind of a cool twist. It makes me unique."

Drake attended Forest Hill Public School when he was young. As he said in an interview with *InterFaith Family*, "I went to a Jewish school, where nobody understood what it was like to

be black and Jewish. When kids are young, it's hard for them to understand the makeup of religion and race," he

Drake with his mother, Sandi Graham

explained. "But the same kids that made fun of me are super proud [of me] now. And they act as if nothing happened." In many ways, Drake believes that being different from other kids made him a stronger person.

Summers were a highlight for Drake. Not only was he out of school for three months, but he often spent that time in Memphis, visiting his father. He learned a great deal about the music culture and about rap musicians from his dad. "Memphis is a place I hold dear to my heart," he told an *MTV News* reporter. He paid honor to those memories of Memphis in his song "Under Ground Kings." Those special summers also helped him maintain a connection with his father. "My dad is a great writer," he told a reporter from *GQ* magazine. "Naturally talented, naturally charming. He embodies that back-in-the-day cool."

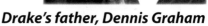

Drake's father, Dennis Graham

Although Drake attended Forest Hill Collegiate Institute for his high school years, he did not graduate. Instead, he followed one of his dreams. For as long as he could remember, he knew he either wanted to be an actor or a musician. When interviewer Claire Hoffman asked him if he had wanted to be an actor when he was a kid, he replied, "That's all I wanted to do, at first. I loved music. I just didn't necessarily believe in music being the focus right away."

With his focus on acting, the chance to become a familiar face on television was just around the corner.

Forest Hill Collegiate Institute

Drake in character, surrounded by the cast of Degrassi

School was a fun place to be for Drake. He was the one who kept his classrooms entertained. As he told *GQ* magazine, "I used to always crack jokes in class. I was a good liar and a good talker. . . . I was my father's son. I was slick, you know? When it comes to knowing what to say, to charm, I always had it."

Although he did not realize it, one of Drake's classmates was doing more than laughing when he watched Drake. He was taking notes. "There was a kid in my class whose father was an agent," Drake recalls. "His dad would say, 'If there's anyone in the class that makes you laugh, have them audition for me.' After the audition, he became my agent."

Drake auditioned for a role in the television series *Degrassi: The Next Generation.* This Canadian show had been on the air for years. It started as *The Kids of Degrassi Street,* which ran from 1979 to 1986. *Degrassi Junior High* followed from 1987 to 1989, and then *Degrassi High* from 1989 to 1991. At only fourteen years old, Drake was hired to play Jimmy Brooks, one of the main characters on *Degrassi: The Next Generation.* This series started in 2001 and was still running more than ten years later.

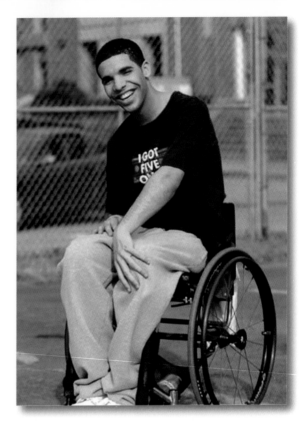

Drake catapulted into stardom with his first role as Jimmy Brooks, creating a huge fan base.

For eight seasons, Drake played the role of Jimmy Brooks. His character was a school basketball star in the beginning, but in the fourth season, Brooks was shot by Rick, an angry fellow classmate. For the next four seasons, Brooks was known as "Wheelchair Jimmy."

Spending all of those episodes in a wheelchair was challenging for Drake as an actor. "Initially, when I found out I was going to be shot and end up in a wheelchair, I spent time with a wonderful kid who was shot and paralyzed," Drake explained in an interview with *The Star Scoop*. "We went places in public and I just wanted to see how people treat you when you're in a wheelchair, and how people treated me for being with someone in a wheelchair, just capture a natural feeling about the overall situation." It did not take Drake long to get accustomed to his new role. "Now, it's just second nature, I don't really have to work that hard at transferring it to Jimmy, because I've been doing it so long that that switch happens," he stated.

Being on a long-running popular show like *Degrassi* was great, but eventually the characters were replaced by a younger set of actors, and Drake found himself unemployed. He appeared in single episodes of a number of other television series, including *Blue Murder, Soul Food, Best Friend's Date, Sophie,* and *The Border,* plus he had a small part as A/V Jones in the movie *Charlie Bartlett* alongside well-known actors Anton Yelchin and Robert Downey, Jr. Despite these roles, Drake was still worried. Was his acting career over? If it was, what would he do next? As he said in a *Biography.com* interview, "I was coming to terms with the fact that . . . I might have to work at a restaurant or something just to keep things going."

Drake needed something else to do, but what? It was time to return to his passion and his heritage: the world of music.

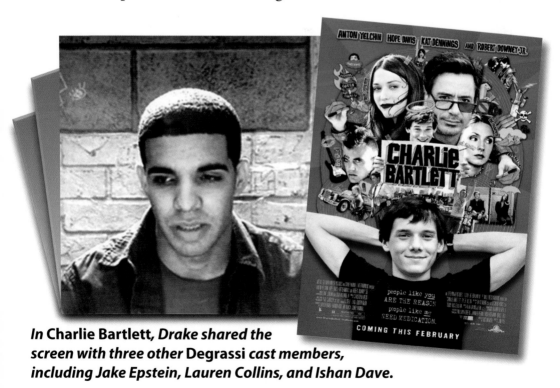

In Charlie Bartlett, Drake shared the screen with three other Degrassi cast members, including Jake Epstein, Lauren Collins, and Ishan Dave.

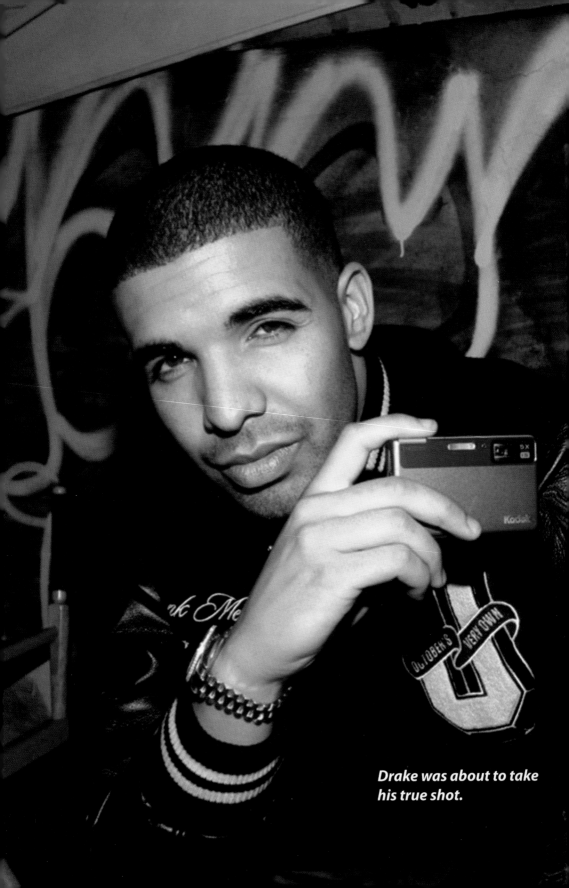

Drake was about to take his true shot.

From Freebies to Fortune

While Drake was acting, he still made it a priority to stay connected with his musical background. Remembering the style of rap musicians his father had introduced him to during those Memphis summers, Drake began doing his own rap, blending traditional styles with singing. As he said in an interview with *The Star Scoop,* "Music is probably my first love. I mean, I love acting. I'll never give it up, but music is definitely something I put my heart into."

In February 2006, he put together his own rap mix tape and uploaded it to his web site. Titled *Room for Improvement,* it featured a dozen songs that he performed and offered as a free download on his blog for anyone who might want it. To his surprise, more than 6,000 people wanted that download.

Inspired, Drake followed up his first mix tape with another free download called "Comeback Season." This one had two dozen songs on it. It was his third mix tape, however, that changed Drake's life. Titled *So Far Gone* and released in early 2009, it was downloaded more than 40,000 times in just 24 hours.

Drake's lyrics in "Best I Ever Had" were dedicated to his female fans. He wrote, "You know a lot of girls be/Thinking my songs are about them/This is not to get confused/This one's for you."

One of the songs on *So Far Gone* was "Best I Ever Had." It was a huge hit with rap and hip-hop fans. By the end of May 2010, the song was in the Top Ten on the R&B/Hip-Hop charts. Just two months later, it was the third most popular song in the country. As Drake told *GQ*, "In order for me to have a working process that doesn't make me crazy, I have to rap about myself. That's the only way I can finish songs. I'm just thankful the world was so receptive to it, because that means I can do it again. And again."

When rap artist Lil Wayne heard one of Drake's mix tapes, he knew that he needed to meet this young man. Drake recalls the moment in *Interview* magazine. "Two songs into [the mix tape], he stopped the CD and asked the person to get me on the phone," he said. Lil Wayne invited the young artist to Houston. "They brought me to my room and I was just in disbelief, like, 'What am I doing here?' You know? For me it was surreal," Drake recalled.

The two musicians got along well. "I think he saw that I was a good kid, or trying to be a good kid," explained Drake, "and I was just staring at one of my idols. I stayed on the road with him for a while, about a week and a half. And I think it was the last night before I went back home, we finally went into the studio and made some music." Drake and Lil Wayne made a demo tape together.

Drake was thrilled to sing on the BET Awards show with his idol, Lil Wayne.

The rest, as they often say, is history. Drake began performing with other popular rap artists, including Jay-Z, Kanye West, Jamie Foxx, and Mary J. Blige. By the end of 2009, Drake had gone from releasing his songs for free online to signing a multimillion-dollar contract with Young Money Records. In 2010, Drake's album *Thank Me Later* was released. It quickly went to number one on the U.S. Billboard Chart, and sold an amazing 447,000 copies in its first week. In 2011, his second studio album, *Take Care,* was released and rapidly climbed the

Drake has worked with some of the biggest R & B singers, including Rihanna.

Drake collaborated with Niki Minaj to record the song "Up All Night."

charts. The two albums contain many hit singles, including "Successful," "Fancy," "Make Me Proud," and "Headlines."

Drake was no longer the class clown or the Canadian TV star. Now he was known throughout the world as a rap star!

Drake's music career has earned him countless awards.

Impressions

By the time he was twenty-five, Drake had already earned his spot in the limelight. He had been nominated for more than 60 awards, including Grammys for Best Rap Song and Best Rap Solo. In 2011 and 2012, he won the title of Songwriter of the Year from BMI (Broadcast Music Inc.) Urban Music Awards. He has also won awards from ASCAP (American Society of Composers, Authors, and Publishers), BET (Black Entertainment Television), and many more.

Some critics have said that Drake's songs are too soft and sentimental compared to most rap music. Admittedly, a number of his songs focus on the ideas of regret over actions taken, self-doubt over decisions made, and sadness over relationships lost. However, Drake defends his tunes in an interview with *Hip Hop Canada*. "I don't want to limit my music to people based on their race and/or age," he explained. "That's why I don't really put a lot of swearing in my music. I want everybody to be able to enjoy it. Being biracial and being young, along with being American and Canadian, [allows me to] try to cover all the bases and expand my fan base to a level that has yet to be seen. I think with the right

Drake wins the BMI Songwriter of the Year award in 2011.

person and the right music, people from all walks of life can come together. I know that's what my life is about. I've seen it all, so that's what I want to bring to the table."

Now that Drake the rapper is far more recognizable than Drake the actor, does that mean he has left acting behind? Not at all. "I've been reading scripts for a while," he told the *New York Post.* "I want to do something great. I want to do something for my culture. The younger people who are still in tune with everything going on."

What other plans does this young star have in place? How about playing one of the most important African Americans in history onscreen? As he told the *Post,* "I hope somebody makes a movie about Obama's life soon, because I could play him. That's the goal. . . . I watch all the addresses. Any time I see him on TV, I don't change the channel. I definitely pay attention and listen to the inflections in his voice. If you ask anyone who knows me, I'm pretty good at impressions."

Besides recording more hit songs, Drake has also appeared in several short films, including *Grimey* and *My Name Is Syn,* and is the voice of Ethan the Mammoth in the movie and game editions of *Ice Age: Continental Drift.* Whether or not he will portray the President of the United States any time soon is unsure, but in the meantime, Drake will keep rapping—and thinking about his future. As he told *Hip Hop Canada,* "I know that Aubrey Drake Graham is not hood. I'm not a gangster. . . . I will talk to you about real situations that I have really been through. I will give

Drake lent his voice to the character of Ethan the Mammoth in the movie Ice Age: Continental Drift.

you pieces of my life, hoping that you will give me time in yours
. . . you know, take the time to listen."

In 2012, Drake reached another goal—he graduated from
high school. This resulted from spending time at the University of
Kentucky (UK) and meeting Coach John "Cal" Calipari and the
Kentucky Wildcats team. In 2009, Drake helped coach one of the
school's intrasquad teams, and the next year, he was there to
cheer them on during an NCAA tournament. When the Wildcats
won the national title, they gave Drake one of their championship
rings. In September 2012, Drake helped coach one of the
Wildcats charity games, helping the team win the game and raise
$350,000 for charity. According to Drake, Coach Cal and UK gave
him "a sense of school, a sense of love, a sense of belonging to
something. That's why I feel like I belong to the UK family. That's
why I'm graduating high school this month. I'm definitely
inspired by UK."

Coach John Calipari played an important and inspirational role in Drake's life.

*The crowd at the **Juno Awards** were thrilled to see Drake and celebrity rocker Justin Bieber together onstage.*

Drake has spent time helping a number of other charities as well. He performed the song "Wavin' Flag" along with artists Justin Bieber, Avril Lavigne, and Nelly Furtado to help raise money for the people of Haiti. He is also a celebrity member of DNA, the charity organization founded by Demi Moore and Ashton Kutcher to help battle sexual abuse. A rumor ran wild on the Internet that Drake would appear in a boxing ring in Las Vegas with Chris Brown to earn money for charity, but it turned out to be a rumor.

Drake has dedicated his life to exploring who he is, while becoming a favorite actor and rapper. Where he might go next is anyone's guess, but you can bet that whatever path he chooses, it will be, as one of his singles says, "Successful."

1986 Aubrey Drake Graham is born on October 24, in Toronto, Ontario, Canada.

1991 His parents divorce.

2001 Drake is hired to play Jimmy Brooks on *Degrassi: The Next Generation.* He will play this role for eight seasons.

2006 He releases his first mix tape.

2009 Drake's third mix tape, *So Far Gone,* snags 40,000 downloads in 24 hours. He meets Lil Wayne and signs a contract with Young Money Records. During Lil Wayne's America's Most Wanted tour, Drake tears his ACL and takes time off for surgery.

2010 Drake's first album for Young Money, *Thank Me Later,* is released.

2011 His second commercial album, *Take Care,* is released.

2012 Drake graduates from high school. He performs charity work to help the people of Haiti.

2013 In June, Drake releases four new songs and announces that his third album, *Nothing Was the Same,* will debut later in the year.

Baby Drake

FILMOGRAPHY AND DISCOGRAPHY

Filmography

2012	*Grimey* (short)
	Ice Age: Continental Drift (voice)
	My Name Is Syn (short)
2009	*Being Erica* (1 episode)
	Sophie (1 episode)
2008	*The Border* (1 episode)
	Degrassi Spring Break Movie (TV Movie)
	Mookie's Law (short)
2007	*Charlie Bartlett*
2005	*Best Friend's Date* (1 episode)
2002	*Conviction* (TV movie)
	Soul Food (1 episode)
2001	*Blue Murder* (1 episode)
2001–2009	*Degrassi: The Next Generation* (TV series)

Discography

Albums

2011	*Take Care*
2010	*Thank Me Later*
2009	*So Far Gone*
2007	*Comeback Season*
2006	*Room for Improvement*

Hit Singles

2012	"HYFR"
	"Take Care"
2011	"Headlines"
	"Make Me Proud"
	"The Motto"
2010	"Fancy"
	"Find Your Love"
	"Miss Me"
	"Over"
2009	"Best I Ever Had"
	"Forever"
	"I'm Goin' In"
	"Successful"

Books

Drake: An Unauthorized Biography. Chicago: Belmont & Belcourt Biographies, 2012.

Shapiro, Marc. *Fame: Drake.* Beverly Hills, CA: Bluewater Productions, 2012.

Torres, John A. *Lil Wayne.* Hockessin, DE: Mitchell Lane Publishers, 2009.

Works Consulted

"Aubrey Graham Exclusive Interview." *The Star Scoop.* December 30, 2007. http://www.thestarscoop.com/music/aubrey-graham-exclusive-interview/

Barchus, Jared. "The Many Sides of Aubrey 'Drake' Graham." *Dr. Guy Presents Musiqology.* November 4, 2009. http://musiqology.com/2009/11/04/the-many-sides-of-aubrey-%E2%80%9Cdrake%E2%80%9D-graham/

Barshad, Amos. "Drake Graham, Black Jewish Hip Hop Star." *InterFaith Family.* June 14, 2010. http://www.interfaithfamily.com/arts_and_entertainment/popular_culture/Drake_Graham_Black_Jewish_Hip_Hop_Star.shtml

Barshad, Amos. "Drake: The Heeb Interview." *Heeb.* June 18, 2010. http://heebmagazine.com/the-heeb-interview-with-drake-the-worlds-first-black-jewish-hip-hop-star/5386

Caramanica, Jon. "Drake Pushes Rap Toward the Gothic." *The New York Times.* November 16, 2011. http://www.nytimes.com/2011/11/20/arts/music/drakes-take-care-goes-to-moody-places.html?pagewanted=all

"Drake Biography." *Forever Drake.* Undated. http://foreverdrake.com/drake/biography/

"Drake [Interview]." *HipHopCanada.com.* July 12, 2006. http://www.hiphopcanada.com/2006/07/interview-drake/

"Drake Wants to Play President Obama." *New York Post.* January 27, 2012. http://www.nypost.com/p/pagesix/drake_wants_to_play_barack_obama_yTGkcmhAQtTHEqkTNR2OaL

Ehrlich, Dimitri. "Drake." *Interview.* Undated. http://www.interviewmagazine.com/music/drake/#_

Eisenberg, Jeff. "Drake Says John Calipari Inspired Him to Finish High School." *The Dagger.* September 17, 2012. http://sports.yahoo.com/blogs/ncaab-the-dagger/drake-says-john-calipari-inspired-him-finish-high-211935690--ncaab.html

Fennessey, Sean. "Rapper of the Year: Drake." *Spin.* June 15, 2010. http://www.spin.com/articles/rapper-year-drake

Hoffman, Claire. "On the Cover: Drake." *GQ.* April 2012. http://www.gq.com/style/gq-100/201204/drake-interview-gq-april-2012

Houghton, Edwin. "Drake's Rise to Fame and Fortune." *The Fader.* September 1, 2009. http://www.thefader.com/2009/09/01/feature-drakes-inscrutable-rise-to-fame-and-fortune

Jurgensen, John. "A Rapper Who Also Sings." *The Wall Street Journal.* November 1, 2011. http://online.wsj.com/article/SB10001424052970204190704577025950950237434.html

Markman, Rob. "Drake Returns to His Second 'Home,' Memphis." *MTV.com.* June 5, 2012. http://www.mtv.com/news/articles/1686618/drake-memphis-second-home.jhtml

Rapkin, Mickey. "Drake Looks for Love." *Elle.* October 13, 2011. www.elle.com/pop-culture/celebrities/drake-looks-for-love-608879

Reid, Shaheem. "Drake Falls Onstage, Reinjures Knee." *MTV News.* August 1, 2009. http://www.mtv.com/news/articles/1617424/drake-falls-onstage-re-injures-knee.jhtml

Rose, Sandra. "The Day Drake Met Weezy: Lil Wayne Takes Over *Interview* Magazine." *SandraRose.com.* March 28, 2011. http://sandrarose.com/2011/03/the-day-drake-met-weezy-lil-wayne-takes-over-interview-magazine/

Tuin, Marian. "Drake's Knee Injury." *Examiner.com.* August 4, 2009. http://www.examiner.com/article/drake-s-knee-injury

Vadnal, Julia. "Drake on 'Thank Me Later.'" *Elle.* July 13, 2010. http://www.elle.com/pop-culture/reviews/drake-on-thank-me-later-454303

On the Internet

Drizzy Drake Online Newsletter
http://www.drizzydrake.org

Forever Drake
http://www.foreverdrake.com

Kidz World: "Drake: Fun Facts!"
http://www.kidzworld.com/article/26875-drake-fun-facts

Young Artists for Haiti: "Wavin' Flag"
http://www.slack-time.com/music-video-8855-Young-Artists-For-Haiti-Wavin-Flag

GLOSSARY

anterior cruciate ligament (ACL)—A tissue that connects the front of the tibia to the back of the femur to help the knee bend.

bar mitzvah—A ceremony to accept a thirteen-year-old boy as an adult member of the Jewish community.

Hanukkah—A Jewish holiday celebrated for eight days.

intrasquad—Within or part of a team.

latke—A pancake, often made from grated potatoes.

mix tape—An individually made tape or CD of specific songs chosen for the receiver.